GOD loves the CHILDREN

Dios Ama a Los Niños

By
Dr. George J. Ceremuga, II, DO
Ambassador for Christ
with decorations and illustrations by
Khai Samante and Ayn Cacha

DR.GEORGEJ, LLC
HOLISTIC HEALTH AND HEALING

ISBN 978-1-63903-889-3 (paperback)
ISBN 978-1-63903-890-9 (digital)

Copyright © 2022 by Dr. George J. Ceremuga

All rights reserved. No part of this publication may be reproduced, distributed, or transmitted in any form or by any means, including photocopying, recording, or other electronic or mechanical methods without the prior written permission of the publisher. For permission requests, solicit the publisher via the address below.

Christian Faith Publishing
832 Park Avenue
Meadville, PA 16335
www.christianfaithpublishing.com

Sharing the content within this book is permissible. Copying or publishing is not permissible.

Printed in the United States of America

Team Love God dedicates this book to the glory of God. We honor and respect all God's children, both big and small. We profess that Jesus Christ is our Lord and Savior. Jesus heals.

Contents

Foreword

Blink your eyes. That is your life on earth when we consider eternity in our heavenly home. Please do not allow any unlove or unforgiveness take away from your blink. That blink was God's gift to you. Blink with love.

Team Love God has brought to the world a reminder that our health (mind, body, and spirit) is our wealth. God never intended medicine to be complicated or messy. Together, we will blaze a trail for the Creator Model of Healthcare powered by the five pillars of wellness to build a healthy, vibrant, and resilient nation as witnesses to the healing power of God's love.

We echo Lakota chief Red Cloud, "We do not want riches, but we do want to train our children right. Riches would do us no good. We could not take them to the other world. We do not want riches. All we want is peace and love."

We are inspired by how "God loves the children." God is gentle, kind, and passionate about protecting them from harm.

Here are three Bible verses where Jesus demonstrated God's love for his children:

Who, then, is the greatest in the kingdom of heaven? He called a little child to him, and placed the child among them. And he said: "Truly I tell you, unless you change and become like little children, you will never enter the kingdom of heaven. Therefore, whoever takes the lowly position of this child is the greatest in the kingdom of heaven. And whoever welcomes one such child in my name welcomes me." (Matthew 18:1–5 NIV)

If anyone causes one of these little ones—those who believe in me—to stumble, it would be better for them to have a large millstone hung around their neck and to be drowned in the depths of the sea. Woe to the world because of the things that cause people to stumble! Such things must come, but woe to the person through whom they come! (Matthew 18:6–7 NIV)

When Jesus entered the synagogue leaders house and saw the noisy crowd and people playing pipes, he said, "Go away. The girl is not dead but asleep." But they laughed at him. After the crowd had been put outside, he went in and took the girl by the hand, and she got up. News of this spread through all that region. (Matthew 9:22–26 NIV)

Indeed, God loves the children. God expects us to train them in peace and love. We welcome each child in your holy name, Jesus.

Lead with love,
Team Love God ♥

Acknowledgments

We acknowledge God's unconditional love for us each day as well as the following:

1. God is the greatest physician.
2. Prayer is the best medicine.
3. We are all responsible for our health and choices.
4. All life and healing come from God.

We all desire to love and be loved. Jesus is all and in all. Jesus Christ is the game changer. Never let go of the hand of Jesus. Love is the fulfillment of the Law.

Introduction

Good day to all our brothers and sisters in Jesus Christ. We are pleased to share our love of Jesus Christ with the world.

Please let me introduce Team Love God: Dr. George, Khai, and Ayn. We have a vision to build a healthy, vibrant, and resilient nation through the power of God's love.

Our mission is to empower one another to the optimal health of our mind, body, and spirit through the Creator Model of Healthcare powered by the five pillars of wellness. We strive to emulate the life of Jesus Christ through humility, love, and forgiveness.

We are honored to be inspired by the Holy Spirit to share our gifts—all gifts are meant to be shared. We will use our family members from the United States and the Philippines throughout the book to share, show, and be love. We are all one in Christ Jesus (Galatians 3:28). We plan a series of books to "unite all in love, for God is love." The first book in our series is in honor of all the children in the world—*Dios Ama A Los Niños*—for God loves the children. We are excited to share with the world the Creator Model of Healthcare, as the glory of God is man fully alive in mind, body, and spirit.

Our tagline is "Lead with love, as the power of love is God." Ready, set, let's go!

Chapter 1

The Greatest Medicine

Dr. George just arrived in the Philippines to visit his friends Ayn and Khai together with their families.

Khai and her daughter, Quisha; her parents, Elvira and Norberto; her brothers, Mark and Jhon; and the couple Ayn and Mike all gathered in Khai's home in Quezon City to have a small welcome celebration.

"Dr. George, I also want to be a doctor one day!" Quisha excitedly said to Dr. George.

"Did you know that *doctor* means *teacher*?" asked Dr. George. "It comes from the Latin *medicus*—to teach."

"Oh! I did not know that, Dr. George. Do you know what the greatest medicine is?" Quisha asked.

With a big smile Dr. George said, "Quisha, that is a wonderful question. Well, would you believe if I say that the best medicine is love?"

Somewhat quizzical, Quisha responded, "Love? Love can heal us from our sickness? But what if that does not work?"

With even a bigger smile, Dr. George said, "Increase the dose. You cannot overdose on love. Unconditional love is the greatest healer. That is the love that God has for us. Nobody can love us as much as God. In fact, God is the Greatest Physician."

Quisha and Dr. George gave each other a big smile and hug.

Chapter 2

Prayer Circle

D r. George called everyone to gather in what he called a prayer circle. *Hmm… I wonder what we will do next.*

"Everyone, please blink your eyes," Dr. George said. "That is your life on earth when you consider eternity in heaven. Please do not let any unlove or unforgiveness take away from your blink. Now what about starting a song to praise our wonderful God?"

Then they joyfully sang songs and praised God!

They sang wonderful songs like "Jesus Loves Me" and "He's Got the Whole World in His Hands," and finally, they sang "Bless the Lord, Oh My Soul."

Chapter 3

Talk to Jesus

Now that they were all warmed up, Dr. George called everyone together and greeted them with a warm smile. He then said, "Good afternoon, my kind brothers and sisters in Christ. Let us inhale love and exhale gratitude: Jesus.

Inhale love, exhale gratitude. JESUS!

This grounding or centering exercise reminds us to stay in the present moment. We can repeat this throughout the day to remind us to always keep our eyes on the prize: Jesus Christ. This constant reminder encourages me to keep my attention and focus on Jesus to help me throughout the day. This allows Jesus to guide my thoughts, words, and actions; and I make better decisions. In essence, I 'talk to Jesus, my guiding light.'"

Keep our eyes on the prize: JESUS CHRIST

"Dr. George, let's all sing together the song that the Holy Spirit inspired you to write, 'Talk to Jesus, My Guiding Light,'" Khai said.

"Sure, Khai," said Dr. George. "Folks, I never was inspired by the Holy Spirit to write a song. And then one May morning this year, as I was driving to turkey hunt, I was inspired to write two songs: one in English, 'Talk to Jesus, My Guiding Light,' and one in Spanish, 'Jesus Sana [Jesus Heals].' So there I was driving down the highway with a pen and notebook acting as the scribe for the Holy Spirit with tears rolling down my face. Two hours later, I was now a singer-songwriter. You never know when and where the Holy Spirit will inspire you. So always be ready."

"Anyone who hears the voice of the Holy Spirit is a prophet," added Ayn. "We were blessed to share this song during our fourteen-day mindfulness moments curriculum. It was extremely helpful during the COVID-19 pandemic to keep in the presence of Jesus, our guiding light."

"Absolutely, Ayn! Silence is the classroom where we hear the voice of the Holy Spirit. Those two songs were gifts given to me by our God during some challenging times. All gifts are meant to be shared. So here we go…" said Dr. George as he started to sing.

19

Talk to Jesus, My Guiding Light

Refrain

Talk to Jesus in the morning
Talk to Jesus in the night
Talk to Jesus my mindful moments
Talk to Jesus my guiding light

Jesus is the Lord of lords
Jesus is the King of kings
Jesus is our salvation
Jesus is in you and me

Refrain

Jesus forgives all our sins
Jesus loves unconditionally
Jesus is totally amazing
Jesus is for you and me

Refrain

Jesus walks with dignity
Jesus talks humbly
Jesus died courageously
Jesus gave his life for you and me

Refrain

Jesus is the Lamb of God
Jesus is the Light of light
Jesus calls us to forgiving
Jesus gives his mercy for you and me

Refrain

Jesus calls us his children
Jesus encourages me to smile
Jesus loves me abundantly
Jesus's presence is peace for you and me

After singing "Talk to Jesus, My Guiding Light," he said, "Yes, my brothers and sisters, Jesus is our guiding light. And his presence is peace for me. I know that Jesus is pleased with our song of praise to him and each other."

Then Dr. George asked everyone to be in the presence of the Holy Spirit and prayed, "Let us all hold hands to make our prayer circle stronger as I open us in prayer. Good and gracious God, we come together before you to give you glory, praise, and honor. We acknowledge you as the Great Physician and prayer as the best medicine. We thank you for your many gifts and blessings, and we are honored to be with our kind brothers and sisters in the Philippines. We pray this in your holy name. Amen."

"Please have a seat and allow me to introduce the Creator Model of Healthcare," said Dr. George. "It is God's model of healthcare, and the medicine of God is free. God loves us so much that he wants us to be just like him. Remember, in the Bible, Genesis 1:27, God created man in his image. In the divine image, he created man and woman."

Elvira agreed and said, "Yes, we were made in God's image. It is time for the world to reclaim the gifts that God has given us. Our bodies are temples of the Holy Spirit [1 Corinthians 6:19]."

"Yes, God expects us to glorify him through our bodies. We are responsible for our health and choices," said Mike.

"Dr. George always reminds us all life and healing come from God," added Khai.

"Indeed," said Dr. George.

Chapter 4

The Five Pillars of the Creator Model of Healthcare

"Dr. George, please share with us the five pillars of God's healthcare model," said Quisha. "I heard that from my mom several times already."

Then Dr. George answered with pleasure, "God gave us everything on earth to be healthy: he created earth for us to have dominion over the plants and animals. The first pillar is water is life. Our bodies are 70 percent water, and we need to drink half our weight in ounces of water daily to maintain health."

"In Lakota, *Mni Wiconi* means 'Water is life.' In Spanish, *Agua es vida*," said Khai. "Yes, water is so very important to the health of our bodies. We should avoid all soda and sugary drinks."

"You are so right, Khai!" Dr. George continued. "And the second pillar is food is medicine. Fruits and vegetables should be the mainstay of our diet, eating the rainbow of colors."

"Hmm… You mean I must be a vegetarian?" Quisha asked.

"Mni Wiconi"
"Agua es vida"
Water is life

"No, honey. We can eat fish, poultry, and lean meats in small quantities. Organic is preferred to avoid pesticides, herbicides, antibiotics, and hormones," Khai explained to her daughter.

"Bravo, Khai!" said Dr. George. "And the third pillar is thirty minutes of exercise on most days. Also, be open to meditative exercise such as yoga, tai chi, or qigong. Motion is a lotion."

"Walking is a great exercise and helps prepare us for sleep, which is the fourth pillar," added Khai. "We should try and get between seven and nine hours of sleep each night to reconstitute and reenergize our bodies."

30-min exercise on most days...

"Absolutely I agree." Dr. George continued, "Sleep is not overrated. We need to control the electronics in our lives and discipline to live all the pillars of wellness, and then sleep should come natural without the need for pills or substances."

7-9 hours of sleep each night

Then Khai stood up and said, "I know the last pillar is the most important, right? It is to be loving and forgiving."

"Yes, Khai," said Dr. George. "Inhale love. Exhale gratitude—Jesus. Keep our eyes on the prize. Love will find a way. Just give it some time. God is love. This pillar is the rock and foundation of God's healthcare model. Unconditional love is the greatest healer. Jesus came to earth to teach us to love, forgive sins, and heal. We are called to do the same, as we are made by God, for God, and to return to God."

"God does love us so much," Elvira added. "He has given us everything for us to live fully alive in mind, body, and spirit. It takes discipline to be a disciple."

"So true, Elvira." Dr. George continued, "As we draw near to God, he draws near to us [James 4:8]. We are guided by the Holy Spirit, and we make better choices for our health and our lives. God's healthcare model is free, and he is available as our health coach twenty-four seven."

"Dr. George, as we close this blessed gathering, let us sing with joy, 'Jesus Sana' in Spanish", said Khai and Ayn. "That is a wonderful idea my kind, talented, and spirit-filled friends," said Dr. George. "Indeed, all for the glory of God!"

Then Mike and Ayn said, "It is so nice that we can take this information and share it with our families and friends. I am glad that we plan to share this with the world, especially with our children. It is our responsibility to teach our children the Creator Model of Healthcare through the five pillars of wellness. Our children are a blessing from God. And Jesus reminds us, 'Therefore, whoever takes the lowly position of this child is the greatest in the kingdom of heaven. And whoever welcomes one such child in my name welcomes me' [Matthew 18:4–5 NIV]."

"Yes, our children are our future, and *Dios amo a los niños*. Right, Quisha?" asked Dr. George.

"Indeed, I love our God!" Quisha cheerfully said.

Jesus Sana: Jesus Heals

(Spanish Lyrics)

Aleluya, Aleluya (suave)
Aleluya, Aleluya (fuerte)
Aleluya, Aleluya (más fuerte)

Aleluya, Jesús sana
Aleluya, cada día
Aleluya, para todos
¡Aleluya, el mundo, amén!

Estribillo:
Aleluya, necesito a mi Jesús
Aleluya, confío en mi Jesús
Aleluya, amo a mi Jesús
¡Aleluya, Jesús sana, amén!

Verso:
Jesús sana, aleluya
Jesús sana, aleluya
Jesús sana, aleluya
¡Aleluya, Jesús sana, amén!

Estribillo:
Aleluya, necesito a mi Jesús
Aleluya, confío en mi Jesús
Aleluya, amo a mi Jesús
¡Aleluya, Jesús sana, amén!

Verso:
Jesús sana, cada día
Jesús sana, cada día
Jesús sana, cada día
¡Cadia dia, Jesús sana, amén!

Estribillo:
Aleluya, necesito a mi Jesús
Aleluya, confío en mi Jesús
Aleluya, amo a mi Jesús
¡Aleluya, Jesús sana, amén!

Verso:
Jesús sana, para todos
Jesús sana, para todos
Jesús sana, para todos
¡Para todos, Jesús sana, amén!

Estribillo:
Aleluya, necesito a mi Jesús
Aleluya, confío en mi Jesús
Aleluya, amo a mi Jesús
¡Aleluya, Jesús sana, amén!

Verso:
Jesús sana, el mundo
Jesús sana, el mundo
Jesús sana, el mundo
¡El mundo, Jesús sana, amén!

Estribillo:
Aleluya, necesito a mi Jesús
Aleluya, confío en mi Jesús
Aleluya, amo a mi Jesús
¡Aleluya, Jesús sana, amén!

Aleluya, Aleluya (suave)
Aleluya, Aleluya (fuerte)
Aleluya, Aleluya (más fuerte)

Aleluya, Jesús sana
Aleluya, cada dia
Aleluya, para todos
Aleluya, el mundo,
amén!
¡Jesús sana!

LEAD with LOVE

Jesus Sana: Jesus Heals

(English Lyrics)

Alleluia, Alleluia (soft)
Alleluia, Alleluia (louder)
Alleluia, Alleluia (loudest)

Alleluia, Jesus heals
Alleluia, each day
Alleluia, for all
Alleluia, the world, amen!

Refrain:
Alleluia, I need my Jesus
Alleluia, I trust my Jesus
Alleluia, I love my Jesus
Alleluia, Jesus heals, amen!

Verse:
Jesus heals, alleluia
Jesus heals, alleluia
Jesus heals, alleluia
Alleluia, Jesus heals, amen!

Refrain:
Alleluia, I need my Jesus
Alleluia, I trust my Jesus
Alleluia, I love my Jesus
Alleluia, Jesus heals, amen!

Verse:
Jesus heals, each day
Jesus heals, each day
Jesus heals, each day
Each day, Jesus heals, amen!

Refrain:
Alleluia, I need my Jesus
Alleluia, I trust my Jesus
Alleluia, I love my Jesus
Alleluia, Jesus heals, amen!

Verse:
Jesus heals, for all
Jesus heals, for all
Jesus heals, for all
For all, Jesus heals, amen!

Refrain:
Alleluia, I need my Jesus
Alleluia, I trust my Jesus
Alleluia, I love my Jesus
Alleluia, Jesus heals, amen!

Verse:
Jesus heals, the world
Jesus heals, the world
Jesus heals, the world
The world, Jesus heals, amen!

Refrain:
Alleluia, I need my Jesus
Alleluia, I trust my Jesus
Alleluia, I love my Jesus
Alleluia, Jesus heals, amen!

Alleluia, Alleluia (soft)
Alleluia, Alleluia (louder)
Alleluia, Alleluia (loudest)

Alleluia, Jesus heals
Alleluia, each day
Alleluia, for all
Alleluia, the world, amen!
Jesus heals!

KEEP YOUR EYES ON THE PRIZE,

JESUS

PLATEAUS OF
PRIDE AND
SELF-WILL

1
LOVE GOD
ABOVE ALL

2
LOVE EACH
OTHER AS GOD
HAS LOVED US

3
ASSIST ONE
ANOTHER ON THE
PATH TO SALVATION

PITS OF SELF-PITY
AND
DESPAIR

THE SACRED PATH

HOLISTIC HEALTH & HEALING

THE CREATOR MODEL OF HEALTHCARE CURRICULUM

GOD'S MEDICINE IS FREE: TO TEACH, TO LOVE, AND TO HEAL

OBJECTIVES:

- Place God first, Jesus did!
- To lead with love - Build a culture of KINDNESS
- Find pure peace in the presence of Jesus
- Empowered to live fully alive in mind body and spirit through the 5 pillars of wellness
- Give God all the glory

VISION:

Build a healthy, vibrant, and resilient nation.

MISSION:

Empower ourselves to the Optimal Health of Our Mind, Body and Spirit through the 5 Pillars of Wellness.

VALUES:

Humility, love, and forgiveness.

GUIDING PRINCIPLES:

- We are all responsible for our health and choices.
- All life and healing come from God.
- God is the greatest physician.
- Prayer is the best medicine.

All we need to fix the world is to *love* one another

THE 5 PILLARS OF WELLNESS PRESCRIPTION:

1 **Water: Mni Wiconi, Agua es Vida, Water is Life (physical and spiritual)**

Drink spring, bottled or filtered water. Half of our weight in ounces.
"...but whoever drinks of the water that I will give him shall never thirst; but the water that I will give him will become in him a well of water springing up to eternal life." -John 4:14

2 **Food is Medicine**

Keep diet simple: whole foods, fruits, and vegetables. Organic if possible.

God said, "I have given you every plant with seeds on the face of the earth and every tree that has fruit with seeds. This will be your food." -Genesis 1:29

3 **Exercise: 30 minutes on most days**

Routine exercise on most days.

Whatever you do, work heartily, as for the Lord and not for men. -Colossians 3:23

4 **Sleep 7 to 9 hours nightly**

In peace I will lie down and sleep, for you alone, Lord, make me dwell in safety.   - Psalm 4:8

5 **Loving and Forgiveness**

Practice love and forgiveness: Imitate the life of Jesus.

You shall love the Lord your God with your whole heart, with your whole soul, and will all your mind. This is the greatest and first commandment. The second is like it: You shall love your neighbor as yourself. -Matthew 22:37-39.

Write positive words that begin with the first letter of your name

①

②

③

④

⑤

CONVERSATION cards

Who is one person you are thankful for and why?

If you could have any super power, which would you choose?

What's one thing you are passionate about?

What are you grateful for?

Share your favorite worship song

What would your perfect day look like?

CONVERSATION cards

What is one way you helped another person today?

What makes YOU unique?

Which three words best describe YOU?

If you could pick your own name what would you pick?

What was the best part of your day?

What is your biggest fear?

QUICK ENERGY TIPS

- Inhale love, exhale gratitude: Jesus

- 4-7-8 Breathing Exercise

- Brain Yoga

- Head, shoulders, knees, and toes

- Drink a large glass of spring water with raw apple cider vinegar, lemon, or lime.

- Close your eyes and place hands on chest.

- Pray: Positive Affirmations

- Go for a walk.

- Important to give and receive 3 hugs daily.

5 Pillars of Wellness

1 Water

Mni Wiconi, Agua es Vida,
Water is Life!

2 Food is Medicine

Fruits and vegetables should
be the mainstay of our diets.

3 Motion is a Lotion

Exercise 20-30 minutes on
most days.

4 Sleep 7-9 hours nightly

5 Love & forgiveness

of self and others.

INHALE
Love
EXHALE
Gratitude
Jesus

Unite all in love for God is love.

God will never leave you nor forsake you.
DEUTERONOMY 31:6

Do everything in LOVE.

1 CORINTHIANS 16:14

Love is FORGIVENESS in action.

45

WE LOVE BECAUSE HE FIRST LOVED US

Smile, Breathe, Love
MEDITATION

SMILE

Relaxes jaw, approachable, open to change.

This meditation can be done throughout the day, reminds us to take time to be still in Jesus' presence.

BREATHE

Breathe in and breathe out. Breathe slowly through your nose and out slowly through your mouth.

Slow our breath to calm our mind, relax our body and renew our spirit which is the foundation for healing.

Use Positive Affirmations:

"I love you, Jesus, I need you, Jesus."
"I run into the arms of Jesus"
"Thank you for your many gifts and blessings."
"Please give me the courage to do your will."
"Relax in my Holy Presence while my face shines upon you."
"Holy Spirit, please guide my thoughts, words, and actions."

LOVE

Unconditional Love is the greatest healer.

The new LOL:
Listen, Obedience, Love

Over time you will automatically slow your breathing, feel more relaxed and find pure peace in the presence of Jesus!
Breathe in Breathe out prior to answering a call, opening a dialogue with a patient, friend, or family member. You will be amazed at how the Holy Spirit will guide you. Many times your choice of words will be softer, kinder, or no words at all.

OUR BODIES ARE temples OF THE HOLY SPIRIT

1 CORINTHIANS 6:19

49

4 GUIDING PRINCIPLES

God created man in his image; in the divine image he created him; male and female he created them.

Genesis 1:27

Truly I tell you, the one who believes in me will also do the works that I do. And he will do even greater works than these, because I am going to the Father. And whatever you ask in my name I will do, to glorify the Father in the Son.

John 14:12,13

We are all responsible for our health & choices.

You must know that your body is a temple of the Holy Spirit, the Spirit you have received from God. You are not your own. You have been purchased at a price. So glorify God in your body.

1 Corinthians 6:19-20

All life and healing come from God.

For I am the Lord who heals you.

Exodus 15:26

Scan the Code!

Scan the code to access our FREE complementary interactive workbook or visit https://drgeorgej.com/free-interactive-workbook/.

Lead with Love as the power of Love is God!
www.DrGeorgeJ.com

Follow Us on Social Media

drgeorgej

@DrGeorgeJCeremuga

@drgeorgej.com

DrGeorgeJCeremuga

About the Author

D r. George J. Ceremuga received a bachelor's degree from the US Military Academy at West Point, New York. He served as an Army officer with the Fourth Infantry Division prior to medical school. He received his doctorate in osteopathy from the Ohio University Heritage College of Osteopathic Medicine and completed a family practice residency at the medical center in Beaver, Pennsylvania.

Dr. Ceremuga then served as an Air Force physician at Ellsworth Air Force Base and finished his twenty-one-year active duty career as a *captain* in the US Public Health Service, serving in rural medical settings on Indian reservations in South Dakota and Montana.

One of his most memorable assignments was as Chief of Integrative Holistic Medicine and Clinical Director of the Fort Belvoir Inpatient Substance Abuse Program from 2013 to 2015. It was during this assignment that the *Holy Spirit* guided his practice to holistic health and healing: empowering ourselves to optimal health through the Creator Model of Healthcare's five pillars of wellness.

Through the Creator Model of Healthcare, his vision is to build a healthy, vibrant, and resilient nation and to share a better way—to teach, to love, and to heal. As an ambassador for Christ, Team Love God's motto is "Lead with love, as the power of love is God."